HYDROPONIC GARDENING FOR BEGINNERS:

A How-To Guide for Growing Vegetables, Herbs & Fruits in Your Own Sustainable Soil-Free Home Hydroponic Garden

BASIL GREEN

© **Copyright 2020 - All rights reserved.**

The content contained within this book may not be reproduced, duplicated or transmitted without direct written permission from the author or the publisher.

Under no circumstances will any blame or legal responsibility be held against the publisher, or author, for any damages, reparation, or monetary loss due to the information contained within this book, either directly or indirectly.

Legal Notice:

This book is copyright protected. It is only for personal use. You cannot amend, distribute, sell, use, quote or paraphrase any part, or the content within this book, without the consent of the author or publisher.

Disclaimer Notice:

Please note the information contained within this document is for educational and entertainment purposes only. All effort has been executed to present accurate, up to date, reliable, complete information. No warranties of any kind are declared or implied. Readers acknowledge that the author is not engaged in the rendering of legal, financial, medical or professional advice. The content within this book has been derived from various sources. Please consult a licensed professional before attempting any techniques outlined in this book.

By reading this document, the reader agrees that under no circumstances is the author responsible for any losses, direct or indirect, that are incurred as a result of the use of the information contained within this document, including, but not limited to, errors, omissions, or inaccuracies.

Download the Audio Version of 'Microgreens' FREE

This book is best enjoyed in its audio format! If you love listening to audio books on-the-go, I have great news for you. You can download the audio book version of this book for **FREE** just by signing up for a **FREE** 30-day audible trial! See below for more details!

Audible trial benefits

As an audible customer, you'll receive the below benefits with you 30-day free trial:

- Free audible copy of this book

- After the trial, you will get 1 credit each month to use on any audiobook

- Your credits automatically roll over to the next month if you don't use them

- Choose from over 400,000 titles

- Listen anywhere with the audible app across multiple devices

- Make easy, no hassle exchanges of any audiobook you don't love

- Keep your audiobooks forever, even if you cancel your membership

- And much more

Go to the links below to get started

FOR AUDIBLE US:

bit.ly/microgreensfree

FOR AUDIBLE UK:

bit.ly/microgreensfreeuk

Before We Begin…

If you enjoy this book then I'd like to ask you for a favor. Would you be kind enough to **leave a review for this book on Amazon?**

It'd be greatly appreciated & will likely help other avid green thumbs with their projects! I read EVERY review I receive and each one helps me to serve each and every one of you better, so your feedback is highly valued!

Thank you,

Basil Green

TABLE OF CONTENTS

TABLE OF CONTENTS 5
INTRODUCTION 1
CHAPTER 1: 3

Hydroponic Gardening: A History and Overview 3

What Is Hydroponic Gardening? 3
The Beginnings of Hydroponic Gardening 4
Hydroponics for the Future 6
Advantages of Hydroponic Gardening 7
Disadvantages of Hydroponic Gardening 11

CHAPTER 2: 13

Practices of Hydroponic Gardening 13

Water Culture vs Medium Culture 13
   Water Culture 13
   Medium Culture 14
   What Are the Hydroponic Growing Mediums? 15
Irrigation and Feeding Techniques 20
   Sub-Irrigation 20
   Passive Sub-Irrigation 20
   Top-Feeding Irrigation 21

Run-to-Waste 21

Recirculating Your Nutrient Solution 23

CHAPTER 3: 25

Understanding Hydroponic Systems 25

Germinating Seeds Without Soil 25

The Six Main Hydroponic Systems 27

Wick System 27

What to Grow 28

Deep Water Culture 29

Variations 30

What to Grow 32

Ebb and Flow 33

What to Grow 34

Drip Systems 34

Variations 35

What to Grow 36

Nutrient Film Technique 37

What to Grow 39

Aeroponics 39

What to Grow 41

Indoor vs Outdoor 42

CHAPTER 4: 45

Step by Step Hydroponic Systems 45

Wick System 45
Deep Water Culture System 48
Ebb and Flow System 51
Nutrient Film Technique 54

CHAPTER 5: 58

Hydroponic Gardening: Nutrients 58

Macro and Micro 58
PH Balance 58
Not All Plants Are Equal 59
Temperature 59
Buy Commercial or Make Your Own 59
Nutrient Ingredients 60
Nutrient Deficiency 61
Nutrient Solution: Balance and Concentration 62

CHAPTER 6: 64

Diseases, Pests, Common Problems 64

Common Problems 64
Water + Nutrients + Light = Algae 64
Leaks 65
Nutrient Deficiencies, pH, EC 65

Hard Water	66
Heat and Humidity	66
Plant Diseases	67
Common Diseases	68
The Solution	68
Plant Pests	68
Common Pests	69
The Solution	69
CHAPTER 7:	**71**
Tips and Myths	**71**
Tips for Hydroponic Gardening	71
Hydroponic Myths Busted!	73
CONCLUSION	**76**
REFERENCES	**77**
BONUS!	**83**

INTRODUCTION

Okay, so you've heard about hydroponics, but what is it and why would you want to try it?

Hydroponics is not a new-age concept, it has been around for a long time, but it is growing in popularity for its soil-free, space-saving, and water benefits. It's not even that difficult to get started with. Kids can do it! You don't need a lot of space, or a garden; it requires no soil. All you need is the time and patience it takes to read this book and you will be well on your way to getting started with your own home hydroponic gardening system.

Hydroponics is a varied genre of horticulture. There are different systems to match different levels of experience and knowledge, right from the absolute beginner to the veteran gardener and even the tech-savvy gardener. There are basic systems you can make from common household items or materials you have lying around the home and garage to fancy systems that require a decent amount of technical know-how. In this book, we will cover all these systems and explain how you can choose and make one of the four simpler systems suitable for beginners.

From page one, we will arm you with all the information you need:

- Understanding the concept of hydroponics and what it is.
- Why it's a great option for urban gardeners.
- How hydroponics is paving the way for the future of agriculture.
- What the different hydroponic systems are.
- How to make your own hydroponic gardening system at

home and some handy tips to help you along the way.

So, now ask yourself this. Are you ready to be stuck in on your journey of growing delicious herbs, vegetables, and fruits right in your own home or garden? If you answered 'yes,' then keep reading as we guide you to your goal every step of the way.

CHAPTER 1:

HYDROPONIC GARDENING: A HISTORY AND OVERVIEW

What Is Hydroponic Gardening?

Hydroponic gardening is often referred to simply as hydroponics. It is a subdivision of what is called hydroculture. Hydroculture is a way of growing plants where they are not grown in soil. Grow plants without soil? That's right! As much as the traditional concept of your hands in the earth and growing plants in soil comes to mind when you think about gardening, you can successfully grow plants out of soil. Instead of soil, hydroponics uses a solution of mineral nutrients dissolved in water to provide the plants with the essential nutrients they need. There are various ways of doing this. Often, the roots are directly exposed to the solution or an immobile substrate other than soil may support them.

Nutrients from a variety of sources may be used in hydroponic systems. Some examples may include chemical fertilizers, duck manure, and artificial nutrients in solutions. Where you get your nutrients from will depend on the type of system you use and what is most readily available to you.

Hydroponics is versatile and allows you to grow a variety of different plants from vegetables, to herbs, to flowers, and even marijuana! A hydroponic garden offers various advantages but comes with its disadvantages as well, all of which we will cover in later sections of this book.

The Beginnings of Hydroponic Gardening

Let's start by dissecting the word hydroponics. It is derived from two root words. The first word is 'hydro', which is English and relates to water. The second root word is 'ponos' which is Greek and relates to work, effort, or labor. Therefore, hydroponics means working with water in a soilless environment to grow plants.

Many people think that hydroponics is a relatively new concept. It may seem futuristic in comparison to the age-old traditional method of growing plants that have been employed since humans discovered agriculture. The truth, though, is actually quite different.

Hydroponic gardening has been around for thousands of years. The ancient world is where it all began. Around 500 B.C.E. King Nebuchadnezzar II gifted his wife, Amytis, with the Hanging Gardens of Babylon, one of the seven wonders of the ancient world. Archeologists and scholars alike have studied the intricate watering systems that supported these legendary gardens for a long time. The way they worked was elevated stonework supporting the plants with central water reservoirs allowing water to flow down over their roots, providing nutrients and aeration. While the hanging gardens are still but a legend, not having yet been discovered by archeologists, their description is clearly an example of hydroponics.

A later example of hydroponic gardening comes in the form of the floating gardens of China, as described by Marco Polo when he documented his travels in the 1300s. Rice is an age-old example of hydroponics as it is grown in water. Initial attempts to grow rice in soil, while difficult, it wasn't unsuccessful. Seasonal floods would decimate other subsistence crops, but rice withstood the waterlogged conditions, and it began to thrive in them. That is where the hydroponic farming of rice paddies in organized fields began. When hydroponic rice farming took off, the rice not only thrived, it also became resistant to more diseases that could possibly plague it, making it hardy and yielding better crops. That's not where the orient stopped with their hydroponics. When Marco Polo documented the use of hydroponics in China, they had developed it to use in growing ornamental gardens.

Hydroponics didn't just stop at providing hardy rice crops; it led to the development of aquaponics. Aquaponics is a system whereby a hydroponic system doesn't just provide a crop harvest above the water; it also supports the farming of fish below the water. Aquaponics has two applications. The first is ornamental, where plants are grown on top of the water. Fishes such as koi are kept in water in spaces like gardens. The other is where crops are grown on the surface and edible fish are farmed below the surface, providing two different sources of food in one body of water.

Another civilization that made use of hydroponics for growing crops is the Aztecs in the 14th to 16th century C.E. The swamp-like regions they lived in, as well as their nomadic way of life, meant that traditional field farming of crops wasn't possible. Instead, they built large floating rafts out of reeds tethered together with dried roots, which would float in the canals surrounding their communities. They would then dredge up silt from the bottom of the canal, which was rich in nutrients, and lay that on top of the rafts. The crops are grown on the rafts and their roots would push through into the water.

As you can see, people have been using soilless systems to grow plants and crops for a long time. However, while there is further documentation of hydroponics throughout history, it wasn't until relatively recently in our modern history that it came to prominence around the world. It wasn't until much later that the concept became popular and intensive research began in order to understand and diversify that concept into what we know today.

In modern times, the earliest recorded reference made to hydroponics was by William Frederick Gericke. In the early part of the 20th century, he started popularizing the concept of growing plants without soil but using water instead. At the time, he was working at the University of California and both his colleagues and the general public were skeptical about his concept of hydroponics. He would go on to prove his claims to be right when he successfully used only water and nutrients to grow 25-foot high tomato vines. He named his concept hydroponics. Since then the concept and application of hydroponics for a variety of purposes, specifically agriculture, has been intensively researched and developed.

Hydroponics for the Future

Hydroponics is increasingly becoming a viable, if not the most viable, way of farming and growing crops. This is because as our global population grows, the amount of usable land for agriculture is declining. Food demands are going up, but the ability to keep up with the demand is slowly declining by the year.

Hydroponic farming allows for the better utilization of space, just like it does with gardening. Farmers will be able to produce more food more efficiently through vertical crop farming, making the most out of less space. This theory can also be applied to your garden in terms of urban farming on a small scale. You rely less on commercial farming when you grow your own vegetables and plants, and just like commercial farming, you can use less space to grow more. This allows you to utilize every bit of space, even vertically, that you have available to you, providing you and your family with delicious, homegrown vegetables.

The other benefit of hydroponics is that it doesn't use nearly as much water as traditional farming and gardening. As our world becomes more populated and more polluted, usable water resources become less. With hydroponics, water is efficiently used and conserved, using less of our precious drinking water supplies as they become scarcer into the future.

Interestingly, NASA is investigating the use of hydroponics to grow fresh food for astronauts in space. Hydroponics could be taking subsistence gardening out of this world.

Advantages of Hydroponic Gardening

As with most things in the world, hydroponics comes with its advantages and disadvantages. Here's what you need to know about the advantages of hydroponic gardening.

No Soil Necessary

Hydroponics work on a soilless system of growing plants. When you don't need soil to grow plants, you can grow plants, such as agricultural crops, in areas that are otherwise unsuitable. It may be because there isn't space, the soil doesn't have enough nutrients, or the land that is available is contaminated.

Space-Saving

When you grow plants in soil, their roots will spread out as they seek food and oxygen. Hydroponics provides a nutrient-rich, oxygenated solution straight to the roots of the plant, meaning that they don't have to expand or compete with each other for nutrients. Hydroponic arrangements allow plants to be planted much closer together, saving space and allowing more plants to grow in the same amount of space.

Natural Elements Aren't a Problem Indoors

When you grow plants outside, they are exposed to elements. Indoor hydroponics has similar advantages to soil-based greenhouses in that you have complete control over the climate your plants are growing in. You can control the temperature, composition of the air, light, and humidity. This allows you to grow plants out of season.

Water-Wise Growing

It's no secret that hydroponic gardening saves water by using only around 10% of the amount of water that traditional soil-based growing uses. Water is used sparingly in many recirculating systems, which means that the plants only take up what they need. The rest runs off, is collected, and the water is circulated back into the system. The only two ways water is lost in these hydroponic gardening setups is through minimal evaporation or leaks in the system.

Nutrients

When you grow plants in soil, depending on the type of plants, only certain nutrients are used, while others aren't. If you plant the same crops or plants repeatedly, the soil becomes depleted of the necessary nutrients for that crop. This is how crop rotation developed. On the other hand, when you use hydroponics you have complete control over what nutrients you put into the solution. You can find out what nutrients are needed for particular plants and how much they need and calculate how much to add to your solution at specific stages of growth. You also don't have the same nutrient loss or change as with soil.

pH Control

Balancing the pH levels in the soil is much more difficult. Using hydroponics, you are able to control the pH levels based on the mineral content of the water, making absorption more efficient.

Plants Grow Faster

When you can control every aspect of an indoor environment that plants grow in, you can create the ideal environment for those plants to grow optimally without much work from the plant. Plants grown with indoor hydroponics don't have to expend precious energy in searching for nutrients and dealing with temperature and light fluctuations. Instead, they can put all their energy into growing.

No Weed Woes

Soil is prone to the annoyance of weeds popping up. Without soil, there are no weeds and no plowing, tilling, etc.

Diseases and Pest Problems Are Less

Hydroponic gardening in a closed and controlled environment lessens the number of pests and diseases associated with soil-grown plants are reduced. If they can't get in or they can't be transferred via soil, they can't be a menace to your gardening. Outdoor hydroponic systems may be somewhat more susceptible to certain pests and diseases compared to indoor systems but without the presence of soil, they are still less prone to diseases than traditional gardening.

Be Gone Herbicides a Pesticides

Since you are removing soil from the equation, many pests and diseases, as well as weeds, associated with traditional gardening are greatly minimized or removed altogether. This means that you don't have to rely on pesticides and herbicides as much as with traditional soil-based gardening. This reduces the amount of harmful chemicals being applied to your plants.

Less Labor, Less Time

With a soilless system, you cut out or minimize tilling, weeding, watering, applying pesticides, manually ridding your garden of pests, testing soil quality, fertilizing, and watering. This, overall, saves you a lot of time and effort.

A Great Hobby

Just as with traditional gardening, hydroponic gardening is a great hobby that allows you to commune with nature. Gardening is a form of therapeutic stress relief, and it offers you tasty rewards when you grow your own veggies!

So, we have extolled the virtues of hydroponic gardening, but what about the negatives that accompany every positive?

Disadvantages of Hydroponic Gardening

It Needs Your Time

Although hydroponics is less labor-intensive and does save time in comparison to traditional gardening, it will still take up some of your time. After all, you are still growing life, tending to it, and cultivating it to be the best it can be. Hydroponics also, unlike their soil-grown counterparts, cannot be left unattended for days or even weeks on end. They need constant care because your system will only keep them going for a short period of time.

Commitment Is Key

You have to be committed to make a hydroponic garden work. You can't leave it alone and hope for the best. You need to learn how it works, discover the nuances about each plant you are growing, and the specific care they need. You have to be committed to being a plant parent and looking after them like a child would need looking after.

Knowledge and Experience

Just as with gardening in soil, hydroponics requires knowledge and experience. You will need to learn how to set up, use, and maintain your equipment. You will have to learn about your plants and their needs and calculate the nutrients, light, temperature, humidity, and more that they will need for optimum growth and health. You will learn through trial and error, and you will gain experience to make you more successful going forward.

Organic or Not Organic, That Is the Question

It is a hotly debated subject whether plants grown using hydroponics are organic or not. The microbiomes that are found in soil may not be the same as with hydroponic systems.

Energy and Water

When using a hydroponic gardening system, water and electricity are used. It is a good idea to make sure everything is set up properly to avoid dangerous situations when water and electricity are in close proximity to one another.

Systems Sometimes Fail

A backup power source is sometimes a good idea when you are using hydroponics for gardening. Depending on how your system is set up, a power outage of several hours could put your plants in jeopardy.

Start-Up Costs

Hydroponic gardening isn't a cheap venture when you really get into it. It takes time and money to set up a good system. Depending on how big or fancy you are going, it could cost hundreds to several thousands of dollars to set your system up. You have the framework, the electrical wiring and pumps, lighting, temperature control, humidity control, and more to budget into the cost of starting up. To start, the costs of basic systems can be quite low. You might even be able to make one using what you have at home, but a solid system for a committed grower is going to cost more. Once set up, your system won't be as costly to maintain, but the initial investment is worth consideration.

Close Quarters

When plants grow in close proximity to each other, which is the space-saving aspect of a hydroponic system, the spread of disease and potential pests is faster than with traditional gardening. We will provide information on pest and disease control for hydroponic gardening later in this book.

CHAPTER 2:

PRACTICES OF HYDROPONIC GARDENING

Water Culture vs Medium Culture

When it comes to hydroponics, there are two main categories to choose from. Water culture and medium culture. Water culture is where there is little to no growing medium, such as soil, which is used for growing plants. The plants are fed an artificial nutrient solution straight to the roots. In medium culture, some form of solid medium, not soil though, is used to grow the plants.

Water Culture

The name water culture can be deceiving. You are not just growing your plants with water but rather a nutrient-rich solution made with water. Another term might be solution culture, but water culture seems to be the one that sticks. There are various types of water culture, but the first decision to make is static water culture or continuous-flow water culture systems. The difference between these two systems is that in a static water culture system the nutrient solution doesn't move and stays in place, while in a recirculating water culture system the solution is constantly on the move. Let's take a closer look at the two methods.

Static Water Culture

When we speak of static water culture, we are talking about a hydroponics practice whereby plants are grown in reservoirs that are filled with a man-made nutrient solution. The point of the static solution culture is the word static. The plants are grown in the reservoir where the solution is kept. They are not grown in a container separate from the reservoir, as is the case with continuous-flow systems. The water is not on the move, so it is not misted, dripped, or flowing over the plant roots and then being recirculated through an external reservoir or allowed to run-to-waste.

Continuous-Flow Water Culture

A continuous-flow water culture is a system whereby the solution is on the move and not static. Plants are grown in containers, which are separate from the reservoir where the solution is kept. The solution can be dripped, misted, or applied to the roots in various ways, but the key point is that the water is moving. This means that continuous-flow culture can be part of a run-to-waste (RTW) system or a recirculating system.

Medium Culture

While hydroponics is known as a soilless way of growing plants, it doesn't mean that a substrate other than soil can't be used. These are known as growing mediums, and various hydroponic systems make use of these substrates. The substrates aid hydroponics in three ways.

Substrates are made of loose particles. As the plant roots grow, they grow between the particles, similar to how plants grow in soil. If you've ever pulled a plant up out of the ground, roots and all, you will notice that it often brings with it clumps of soil. This is because the roots have grown between the soil particles and the finer parts of the root system have trapped the soil particles like a mesh net. What this does when roots grow between substrate particles is that it helps to aerate the roots, offering them ample opportunities to get enough oxygen.

Substrates retain moisture. Even if the solution has been passed through the substrate, it will retain some of that solution, providing plants with the opportunity to draw that nutrient-rich solution from the substrate continuously. It also helps to keep the plant roots damp, stopping them from potentially drying out. Again, this emulates the way plants grow in soil. When you water your garden or houseplants, the water passes through the soil, but the soil retains some of the water for them to draw up over time.

Finally, substrates help to insulate your plant's roots. This is important because it protects them from heat, which could potentially damage them.

What Are the Hydroponic Growing Mediums?

Rockwool

One of the more popular growing mediums, rockwool, is non-degradable and made up of mainly granite but may contain limestone as well. These are superheated until they melt and then they are spun into thin, wool-like threads similar to cotton candy or sheep's wool.

Caution: When using rockwool, ensure that it never becomes saturated. It soaks up water fast and could suffocate your roots or cause stem and root rot. Rockwool needs to be pH balanced, so soak it in some pH-balanced water before you use it.

Hydrocorn

Hydrocorn is also known as grow rock and it is a lightweight expanded clay aggregate (LECA). This means that clay that has been super-fired in order to create porousness. It's lightweight enough so that it doesn't squash your plant roots but at the same time heavy enough to offer support. Hydrocorn has a neutral pH balance and is ideal for both retaining moisture and wicking moisture upwards towards plant roots. This growing medium is reusable, but you will have to clean and sterilize it before reuse.

Coco Fiber/Coco Chips

Coco fiber, also known as coco coir, and coco chips are made from outside husks of coconuts. Even though coco fiber is an organic, biodegradable product, it does so very slowly, and it won't contribute any nutritional value for your plants. It retains water well and is pH balanced. The difference between coco fiber and coco chips is the size of the substrate particles. The particle size of coco fiber is roughly the same as potting soil, while coco chips are roughly the size of wood chips. The benefit of coco chips is that their larger size offers better aeration at the root level.

Perlite

Perlite is primarily made up of minerals that have been significantly heated until they expand almost like how heated corn kernels pop into popcorn. This means that this substrate is lightweight, porous and absorbs liquid well. Not only does it retain water well, but it also acts as a good wicking agent. Because perlite is so lightweight, it floats and thus is not the best option for ebb and flow hydroponic systems.

Caution: Wet perlite down before you work with it so that the dust doesn't become airborne and get into your eyes.

Vermiculite

Similar to perlite, vermiculite is a silicate mineral. Likewise, it is heated and expands. Vermiculite is very similar to perlite in its ability to store nutrients to be used later. Just like perlite, it is very lightweight and not suitable for ebb and flow systems.

Caution: Vermiculite comes in different types for different uses. Be sure to use the type that is intended for use in horticulture.

Oasis Cubes

Similar to rockwool cubes and having similar properties but not appearance, oasis cubes are more akin to white or green floral foam. The material is what is called open-celled, which means that the cells can absorb air and liquid. It is also a good wicking agent and because of the open cells, the roots of the plants can easily expand and grow. Oasis cubes are traditionally used as a start to growing plants in hydroponics but can be used as substrate as well.

Caution: As with rockwool, oasis cubes absorb water quickly and easily, so be careful not to saturate them so that you won't suffocate the plant roots or end up with stem and root rot.

Floral Foam

Similar to oasis cubes, floral foam is an open-cell growing medium. However, the size of the cells is larger than oasis cubes. You may enter a few problems if you are going to use floral foam. It crumbles easily which can cause particles to get into your nutrient solution and contaminate your reservoir if you have a recirculating system. Like oasis cubes and rockwool, you don't want it to become saturated. It will have the same effect of suffocating your roots or causing root and stem rot.

Growstone

Recycled glass is used to make growstone. It is dust-free and lightweight. It also provides good aeration to the roots by creating large air pockets between the stones. Growstones are porous and offer a good wicking capability. Being able to wick water up to four inches above the waterline means that you will want good drainage in place or a deep layer of this substrate.

River Rock

River rock is easy to find and a common product in home improvement stores and pet supply stores. It is a relatively cost-effective substrate option. They do not retain water well as they are not porous, and their size provides many large air pockets between the rocks. You will want to feed often with your nutrient solution so that the plant roots don't dry out.

Caution: If you are using river rock as a substrate, try mixing in coco chips to help with moisture retention and minimize the drying of roots.

Pine Shavings

Inexpensive and utilized by many commercial growers, pine shavings are a good option for bigger home hydroponic gardening setups. As pine shavings are wood, they have good absorption but can easily become waterlogged.

Caution: Ensure that you use pine shavings and not sawdust. Also, make sure that the source is kiln-dried wood and that it does not have any chemical fungicides in it. Make sure that the pine shavings have good drainage and don't become waterlogged or you could end up with root problems.

Aged Composted Pine Bark

Pine bark is often considered a better option than many other tree bark substrates. It doesn't decompose as quickly and easily and contains a lesser amount of organic acids, which could possibly contaminate your nutrient solution.

Polyurethane Foam

Not commonly used in hydroponic gardening, polyurethane foam can sometimes be used as an alternative to rockwool. It is cost-effective and not hard to come by; it is often called foam batting.

Water-Absorbing Crystals

Water-absorbing crystals are not new and are not common for hydroponics. Polymer crystals that absorb water are used in many applications. One application has been in traditional gardening where these crystals are mixed into the soil to help with moisture retention. They expand greatly, and as much as 50 gallons of water can be retained in only one pound of crystals. They come in a variety of sizes from resembling a powder to the size of a marble, or the size of a golf ball. Depending on how big the crystals are, they can take up to two hours to absorb their full amount of water. They resemble jello when they are saturated. They are reusable once completely dried out and can then be easily stored.

Caution: When used on their own, because of their expansion and moldable nature when they are saturated, these crystals could cause problems with providing an adequate oxygen supply to roots.

Sand

Not to be confused with soil, sand is a common growing medium for hydroponic gardening. Similar to rock, the only difference being its tiny pint-sized particles, it doesn't drain water as quickly. You can easily, and this is common practice when using sand as a substrate, mix it with the likes of coco fiber, perlite, and vermiculite.

Tip: Use the largest size of sand grain you can find as this increases aeration.

Caution: Sand can be very heavy as a growing medium for hydroponic gardening. Mixing it with other substrates helps lessen the load but always be careful.

Rice Hulls

Your location will dictate whether rice hulls are easily accessible. Being an organic substrate isn't a problem as rice hulls degrade very slowly. Rice hulls are commonly added to a mix of growing mediums as opposed to being used as a stand-alone substrate. They generally have the correct pH-balance, which is a bonus.

Caution: Ensure that you use parboiled rice husks (PRH) because when it is fresh it could contain contaminating pathogens.

Irrigation and Feeding Techniques

In this section, we will discuss the two types of irrigation: run-to-waste and recirculating. These irrigation techniques don't necessarily have anything to do with how the nutrient solution is provided to the plants, such as dripping or misting, but rather with how the solution is managed. In addition to solution management irrigation practices, we will also discuss sub-irrigation and top-feeding irrigation.

Sub-Irrigation

As the name implies, sub-irrigation is the method of providing a nutrient solution to your plants from below. Examples of hydroponic systems, which make use of sub-irrigation are deep water culture, ebb and flow, nutrient film technique, and the wick system. In these systems, the nutrient solution is provided to the plants from below. The plant roots rest in the solution or the solution is transferred upwards towards the roots through the substrate. The key is that the solution is provided at or below the root level.

Passive Sub-Irrigation

Passive sub-irrigation is also known as semi-hydroponics or passive hydroponics. It uses a substrate to grow the plants in.

These substrates are porous and allow water to be transferred upwards to the plant roots. A separate reservoir is used for the nutrient solution, placed below the substrate so that the roots are not directly in contact with the solution. Passive sub-irrigation is a form of static solution culture.

A simple but effective example of passive sub-irrigation is to use a substrate or growing medium, such as grow rock, which is porous and has a good wicking capability. Take a plastic soda bottle and cut it horizontally in half. Fill half of the bottom half of the bottle with a nutrient solution. Remove the cap and flip the top half of the bottle upside down. Insert a wicking material to use as a wick, such as cutting a cotton sock into strips, through the upside-down bottleneck so that half the wick strips are inside the bottle and the other half is sticking out the bottleneck. Place the upside-down top half of the bottle into the bottom half, fill it with your substrate, sow your plant and start growing. The solution will be transferred to the substrate by the wicks and then the substrate will carry it further up to the plant roots.

Top-Feeding Irrigation

In a top-feeding irrigation system, the nutrient solution is provided to the plants from above the root level. Hydroponic systems that use this type of irrigation include drip systems and top-feeding deep water culture systems. The solution is applied from above and moves downwards, often through a growing medium or substrate.

Run-to-Waste

Run-to-waste (RTW) in a hydroponic system, also called feeding-to-waste or drain-to-waste, is exactly what it sounds like. In this irrigation practice, plants are typically grown in a substrate with good liquid retention capabilities. The nutrient solution is passed along through the substrate and excess solution runs off or drains to 'waste' in a catchment container separate from the reservoir. This is a concept similar to how soil functions. Water passes through the soil, allowing plants to absorb water as it passes the roots. The run-to-waste irrigation practice may seem wasteful, as the name implies, but it does have both advantages and disadvantages.

Advantages:

- Nutrients don't become depleted in the solution because a fresh solution is provided with each feeding. This means you do not have to monitor the reservoir solution's nutrient levels or top them up.
- The electroconductivity (EC) of the nutrient solution in the reservoir remains constant.
- The pH balance of the solution remains constant.
- The maintenance of a run-to-waste irrigation system is lower than a nutrient recirculating system.
- The solution is not as prone to a build-up of pathogens such as bacteria.
- The liquid retention capability of the substrate used keeps the roots of the plants moist and thus helps guard your plants against an electrical failure, which could disable the solution supply.
- The substrate acts as insulation, protecting the plant roots against heat.

Disadvantages:

- Uses more water.
- Uses more nutrients, which adds to the costs.
- Nutrient leaching may happen more frequently.

- You may experience salt accumulation.
- This irrigation practice is only applicable to some hydroponic systems.

Recirculating Your Nutrient Solution

The opposite of run-to-waste is recirculating your nutrient solution. In a recirculating system, the plants are provided with the nutrient solution. The excess that runs off is then recaptured and circulated back into the reservoir to be used again. This may seem like a smarter practice than run-to-waste but there are both positives and negatives.

Advantages:

- The nutrient solution is recycled, losing less water and nutrients.
- Nutrient leaching is reduced.
- The amount of nutrients you use may be reduced.
- Several hydroponic systems may be run on a recirculating irrigation practice.

Disadvantages:

- Water-borne diseases are more common and spread like wildfire.
- Nutrient levels of the solution will fluctuate as plants absorb the nutrients in the quantities they need. This leads to the solution becoming depleted, which will require constant testing and management of nutrient levels.
- The pH and electroconductivity of the solution may fluctuate which will require testing to manage and maintain at appropriate levels.

- Algae growth is more likely, and drip emitters may become blocked with biofilm or algae.

CHAPTER 3:

UNDERSTANDING HYDROPONIC SYSTEMS

Before we get into the different hydroponic systems and how they work, let's start with a quick guide on how to germinate the seeds into the seedlings you will be planting in these systems.

Germinating Seeds Without Soil

The simplest and most convenient way to get seedlings for your hydroponic system is to go to the local nursery and buy seedlings that have already been germinated and have started growing. There are three drawbacks to this approach.

- You haven't had control over the quality of nutrients the seedlings have received from day one, so you haven't been able to control whether they got the best start in life or not.

- You may be quite limited in what you can grow according to what seedlings are available.

- Let's face it, that sense of pride and self-satisfaction that you get from germinating your own seeds is worth the effort, and you really don't get that from buying seedlings.

Okay, so we've convinced you to give germinating your own seedlings a try. Now, how do you do it?

- Choose your germinating medium. The two most popular choices are coco peat and rockwool cubes. Both are good choices for germinating seeds with a neutral pH and a good water to oxygen ratio.

- Once you have chosen your germinating medium, prep it by letting it stand for a few hours in distilled water.

- Drain excess water out of your germinating medium by lightly shaking it.

- Place a few seeds into your medium. You want to use a few seeds per piece of germinating medium in case some don't sprout. If you want to, you can always separate or remove any extra sprouts later.

- Put your growing medium in a shallow container with a cover. Set it aside in a safe, dark place until sprouting begins, which usually starts in about five to seven days.

- During the germination phase, ensure that the germinating medium stays damp but not drenched. If it is too wet, it will be soggy and fall apart. Keeping it at the right moisture level will help get the best germination results. Start off with distilled water. You can begin adding small amounts of nutrients later on or you can wait until your seedlings reach a height of two inches. After, start providing the mix of nutrient solution you would feed adult plants that has been quite diluted. If you test the EC of the seedling solution, it shouldn't have a reading above 8-1.2.

- Once your seeds have germinated, they will enter the propagation stage where they start growing and becoming stronger. Once your seedlings have developed stronger roots and about three sets of proper leaves, they are ready to be transplanted into your hydroponic system where they will live out the rest of their lives.

Tips

- Don't let the germinating medium dry out.
- Don't let the germination container be affected by

extremes in temperature variations. Research what temperatures are best for germinating the seeds you are going to grow and try to keep the container at that general temperature.

- After transplanting your seedlings into your hydroponic gardening system, water them with nutrient solution from the top for a week or so to allow the roots to grow downward and prevent drying out.

The Six Main Hydroponic Systems

In hydroponics, there are six main systems. Each system has its benefits and drawbacks. To choose the right system for your needs and the plants you want to grow, you need to understand how each system works.

Wick System

The wick system is one of the simplest hydroponics systems and it is a good place for beginners to start. It is known as a passive system, meaning that there are no moving parts to this system. Passive sub-irrigation is what the wick system makes use of for irrigating your plants. The plants are grown in a container filled with substrate above the reservoir, and there are wicks that hang down from the substrate container into the reservoir. The wicks carry the nutrient solution up to the substrate or growing medium, which is where the plants then draw their nutrients and water from.

A wick system is the simplest hydroponic system by far and can be seen as a training stepladder to bigger and better systems. It is so easy that you can literally make it out of ordinary household items or by upcycling or recycling items you would otherwise normally chuck in the trash.

The one thing to consider in your setup is whether you are going to use an air pump or not. It is an optional addition to your wick system, so it isn't necessary, but it can be beneficial. Your plants should be able to take up oxygen from the air pockets in the substrate it's planted in and from the water the nutrients are mixed with. However, providing more oxygen isn't a bad idea. Not only does using an air pump boost the oxygen level on the solution, it also helps keep the solution swirling and moving. This constantly mixes up the nutrients and prevents them from setting at the bottom of the reservoir.

Advantages of the wick system:

- It is easy and cost-effective to build.
- It is easy to maintain, making it ideal for beginners.
- It doesn't require large energy inputs.

Disadvantages of the wick system:

- Unsuitable for larger plants that need to draw up more water.
- Nutrient delivery isn't very efficient. The wicks can't tell how much of what nutrients the plant needs and just transports everything equally to the growing medium. The plant takes up as much of the necessary nutrients as it needs and leaves the rest behind in the substrate, which can cause a potentially toxic buildup of nutrients.

What to Grow

A wick system is a good idea if you are planting small, non-fruit-bearing plants. This system cannot support water-hungry plants or plants that need larger amounts of nutrients. It cannot supply enough water and nutrients to those plants and it cannot do so quickly enough.

Your best plant choices are plants that are relatively small in size, light on water and nutrients such as lettuces and herbs.

Deep Water Culture

Deep water culture (DWC), also referred to as direct water culture, and is a system of hydroponics where your plants are suspended over a reservoir of a well-oxygenated nutrient solution. The roots of the plant are submerged in the solution. There are two reasons this system got its name. Firstly, the reservoir used should be able to hold a fair amount of solution. Secondly, much of your plant root mass is constantly submerged in the solution almost all day long. This is unlike other systems, which may wet or drench the roots several times a day, leaving the roots exposed to the moisture-retaining substrate in between.

Deep water culture is a popular hydroponics system for beginners as it is relatively easy and inexpensive to set up and use. The only hydroponics system that is even easier and simpler to use is the wick system.

Advantages of Deep Water Culture:

- Once you are set up, this system is quite low maintenance.
- Compared with traditional soil growing, a deep water culture system allows plants to grow much faster.
- Putting together a deep water culture system is easy, and there are relatively few moving parts involved.

Disadvantages of Deep Water Culture:

Some disadvantages may be circumnavigated through proper hydroponic garden maintenance.

- Fluctuations in pH, nutrient concentration, and the level of the solution in the reservoir can fluctuate greatly in smaller systems.
- If you are working with a smaller system, due to the small scale of the system, it can either be extremely easy to under or over calibrate your nutrient solution.
- If your air pump fails or you have an electricity outage, the roots of your plants may 'drown' if there isn't enough oxygen being pumped into the solution.
- Maintaining a constant water temperature can be a bit of a headache.

Variations

When it comes to deep water culture systems, there is more than one to choose from to suit your specific growing needs.

Traditional Deep Water Culture

A traditional deep water culture system is often where newcomers to hydroponics start out. These systems are easy to set up, easy to maintain, and don't break the bank. They also offer you the option to expand at a later stage into a modular or recirculating deep water system. These systems utilize either a floating raft concept or gaps for plant containers that are cut into the container lid. Plants are placed in holders or on the raft with their roots suspended in the nutrient solution. An air pump and air stone aerate the water that prevents plant suffocation. The advantage of opting to go with the floating raft concept is that as the water level drops, so does the raft, which ensures that your plant roots are always suspended in the solution. If you opt for placing plant holders in the lid of the container, pay careful attention to the level of the solution so that it does not drop lower than the roots can reach.

Static vs Recirculating

This question is the same as asking whether you should have a singular or modular deep water system. The answer is simple. If you are new to hydroponics, it's best to start simple with a singular or static system. A singular or static system is one in which each plant or cluster of plants is in its own reservoir of nutrient solution, separate from other plants or plant clusters and reservoirs. You may have multiple reservoirs to grow multiple plants or plant clusters at the same time, but they are all separate from each other. This does bring in a bit more work because each separate reservoir needs to be tested for pH and nutrient concentration.

Modular or recirculating deep water systems link several containers with the same type of plants together and to a central reservoir. The nutrient solution is then circulated through all the containers and back to the main reservoir continuously. You can monitor the main reservoir for pH levels and electroconductivity or nutrient levels instead of testing each plant container separately.

Recirculating or modular deep water culture systems are something you can look into as you gain experience, knowledge, and can better manage a larger, slightly more complex system.

Top-Fed Deep Water Culture

Top-fed and traditional deep water systems are not that different. In both systems, the plant roots hang down towards the reservoir of the solution. With a top-fed system the oxygen-rich solution is pumped up from the reservoir and released directly on the roots of the plant and from there flows back into the reservoir.

The advantage of this over a traditional system is that within the first few weeks of the seedlings' growth the roots are still growing towards the reservoir in traditional systems. This leads to a slower growth rate, whereas a top-fed system allows sooner access to the nutrient solution, which aids in faster growth. Once the roots of the plants reach the reservoir below, both systems are equally matched.

Bubbleponics

The name might sound a little silly, but bubbleponics can be advantageous in the first few weeks of growth. With bubbleponics, you are using a regular deep water culture system, adding a water pump and drip tubes. The water pump will pump the water up to the top of the reservoir where drip tubes will drip feed the young plants until their roots grow down into the reservoir. This top feeding technique that speeds up the growth in young plants, much the same way as a top-fed deep water system does.

What to Grow

Deep water culture systems making use of the raft system can only support lighter plants. Larger plants and top-heavy fruit-bearing plants aren't suitable for this hydroponics system. If you are using a deep water system whereby your plants are in holders fitted into the lid of the container, the plants can be slightly heavier.

Good crops for deep water systems include:

- Bok Choy/Tatsoi
- Lettuce
- Basic
- Okra
- Collard greens
- Kale
- Chard

- Sorrel

Ebb and Flow

Ebb and flow hydroponic systems are also known as flood and drain systems. These systems work by growing plants in a substrate that is in a container above the reservoir. A timer is set, and a water pump pumps the solution into the plant container, flooding it. As the plant container or tray floods, an outlet makes use of gravity to allow the solution to drain back into the reservoir, and this flooding and draining cycle carries on at regular intervals.

Ebb and flow systems are seen as an intermediate hydroponic system that is not only easy and cost-effective to set up but also quite versatile. Ebb and Flow systems may or may not require an air pump to aerate the solution. This depends on how your system is set up.

Advantages of ebb and flow:

- East to set up and cost-effective.
- Easy to use and maintain.
- Sufficient nutrients provided to the plants.

Disadvantages of ebb and flow:

- Malfunction of equipment could leave your plants either high and dry or drowning in the flood phase.
- pH level fluctuations due to the flooding and draining process.
- Potential salt buildup caused by the flood and drain process.

What to Grow

You can grow larger plants and fruit-bearing plants in an ebb and flow system as opposed to a wick or deep water culture system. Some crops that do well in ebb and flow systems include:

- Lettuce
- Tomatoes
- Cucumbers
- Celery
- Watermelon
- Cantaloupe
- Oregano
- Chives

Drip Systems

A drip system is also referred to as a trickle system or a micro-irrigation system. How this works is just as it sounds. A pump will pump nutrient solution through drip tubing and dripping the solutions onto the plants directly. This is not a concept that is unique to hydroponics and has been around for a while as part of traditional soil-based gardening.

Using a drip system allows you to feed your plants slowly, manage water-loss more effectively, and have a greater control over the amount of water and nutrients your plants receive. A drip system consists of a network of tubing and lines and is usually more suitable to larger hydroponic setups, which is often the preferred hydroponic system used by large-scale growers and farming.

The drip system works by either having individual plants in separate pots of substrate or several plants in a tray of growing medium. Each plant has its own dedicated emitter dripping solution onto it. Drip tubing connects the plants to the reservoir and there are two ways to use pressure to supply the solution to the plants. You can use a pump to pump the water or a system that relies on gravity to do the hard work.

The emitters in your system allows you to have full control over the flow of the solution and how much and how quickly your plants are fed. This is what makes a drip system so versatile. You can adjust the levels of flow according to what plants are being irrigated by those specific emitters.

When you use a drip system, the flow needs to be controlled so that the substrate you are using gets an opportunity to breathe in between irrigation sessions. If you leave your drip system unattended and unregulated, you could end up eventually flooding and suffocating your plants. Timers are an essential part of drip systems, for this reason, and you can set specific times of day for the pump to work and shut off to feed your plants in intervals.

A drip system is not an absolute beginner system. It is something to aspire and work your way towards as you gain knowledge and experience, but it takes a lot of planning and careful installation to get it just right. Once you have a drip system set up, running and maintaining it is easy.

Variations

There are two types of drip systems. Recirculating or recovery systems and non-circulating or non-recovery systems. The variation you choose to use comes down to personal choice.

Recirculating/Recovery Drip System

Recirculating drip systems allow the excess nutrient solution that is not absorbed to circulate back into the reservoir. This is popular with smaller home hydroponic setups as it saves water and nutrients. However, there are drawbacks to consider:

- When the run-off nutrient solution is recycled back into the reservoir, it alters the pH balance in the reservoir, which leads to you performing a periodic maintenance on the recirculation system.
- You will have to monitor the pH balance and nutrient concentration of the reservoir regularly to ensure that the correct levels are maintained.

Non-Circulating/Non-Recovery Drip System

A non-circulating drip system operates on the opposite principle to the recirculating variant. This system takes a run-to-waste approach, allowing the excess run-off solution to be collected in a catchment and discarded.

This is not always an effective way of working since it doesn't conserve water or nutrients. However, when using a drip system, run-off is minimal. Non-circulating drip systems are popular with bigger commercial growers who use advanced timing systems to maximize control over their flow and keep wastage to a bare minimum. Not recirculating the waste solution also means that they don't have as much reservoir maintenance to do.

What to Grow

- Pumpkins
- Lettuce
- Onions
- Leeks
- Peas
- Melons

- Radishes
- Tomatoes
- Strawberries
- Cucumbers
- Zucchinis

Nutrient Film Technique

The nutrient film technique (NFT) is a popular and simple hydroponic system that is not entirely different to the ebb and flow system with a different layout. This system is often used to grow plants that are smaller and grow faster.

There are different layouts for a nutrient film hydroponic system, but all of them have certain similarities. All NFT systems are based on a nutrient solution that is kept quite shallow as it pours down through a tube that is typically slanted. The plant roots take the water and nutrients they need as they are exposed to the solution.

Both the ebb and flow system and the nutrient film technique use pumps to bring the nutrient solution to your plants. However, unlike the ebb and flow system, the NTF system does not flood your plants with the solution. Instead, in a nutrient film technique system, the solution is continuously flowing and recirculating through the plant roots.

The NTF system is active, and this means it needs moving parts to run. It isn't passive like a wick system, which works slowly. This is why the nutrient film technique is effective for fast-growing plants.

The design of the NFT system is simple and, if you have the knowledge, not too hard to replicate.

This system consists of two main parts. The channel or the tray in which the plants are grown and the nutrient solution reservoir.

Net pots holding the plants are placed in the channel or grow tray. Each net pot contains a substrate, and the plants are grown in that substrate. As the plants grow, their roots grow downwards to the bottom of the channel where the solution is flowing past. It is also possible to forgo the substrate and just place the plants directly into the net pots after germination and propagation.

A pump has to be employed to pump the water along the channels and past the plant roots. The solution then flows into the drainage system to be recycled back into the reservoir and cycled through the system again.

How this system works is that the channel is positioned at an angle. The pump moves the solution to the highest point of the grow tray. It then flows down to the lowest angle where it is recirculated through a waste or return pipe back into the reservoir. The channel being at an angle negates the need for a secondary pump to help return the excess solution to the reservoir. Gravity does all the work.

As the roots are entirely exposed, they are able to take up enough oxygen, and being partially submerged in a shallow layer of moving nutrient solution lets the plants take up enough water and nutrients.

Advantages of NFT:

- Water and nutrient consumption is relatively low.
- You don't actually have to use growing media.
- It's easy to clean and disinfect the setup.
- Buildup in the root area is prevented due to the continuous flow.

- Water-loss is minimized due to the recirculation of the solution.
- The system is expandable and modular because of its customizable concept.

Disadvantages of NTF:

- If your pump fails to operate due to technical issues or electrical outages, your plants can die very quickly.
- Plants with large taproot systems aren't suitable.
- Plants requiring root support are not suitable.

What to Grow

Various plants can be grown in a nutrient film technique system. The criteria is that they are fast growing and lightweight. Because the roots don't offer much support for the plant, this system is not suitable for larger, heavier plants that need that level of foundation. Some vine plants, such as tomatoes and squash, can be grown in this system using a separate trellis system to support the weight of the fruit as they develop.

Aeroponics

Aeroponics may sound like something futuristic out of a sci-fi novel, but it really isn't. The concept is simple enough, and the system isn't too difficult to build if you have the technical knowledge and experience. However, the truth is that this system is the most complex of the six basic hydroponic systems and is best left alone until you have more knowledge and experience.

An aeroponic system can be made out of a variety of materials, depending on what you have available, your budget, and how you design your system. Many people choose to build their own systems.

An aeroponic system works in an environment where the roots are entirely enclosed. The roots of the plants are continuously or periodically misted with a nutrient-rich solution. The environment is enclosed to prevent moisture loss and aid in minimizing wastage. The plants are partly divided between worlds. Half the plant is above the surface of the reservoir container, allowing it light, oxygen, etc. The root system is below the top of the reservoir, being misted with the solution.

A simple example of an aeroponic system would be if you took a container and cut holes in the top to place net pots to hold the plants. The system inside that enclosed container would allow for misting to occur through spray nozzles. All excess solution would drip back to the bottom of the reservoir container to be recycled and misted again. This is a very simple explanation. The mechanical workings behind it are much more complex, but you get the idea behind it.

Advantages of aeroponics:
- Accelerated plant growth.
- Maintenance of the system is relatively easy once it is set up.
- Lower water and nutrient needs.
- Aeroponic stations are relatively mobile compared to other systems.
- Aeroponic systems are moderately space-saving.

Disadvantages of aeroponics:

- System dependency means that if the system fails, the plant roots will dry out and die.
- Requires technical knowledge and experience.
- The container the plant roots are housed in needs regular cleaning.
- Prohibitive cost.

What to Grow

- Strawberries
- Lettuce
- Basil
- Tomatoes
- Mint
- Leafy greens
- Herbs

Indoor vs Outdoor

The indoor versus outdoor debate is a big question when you enter the world of hydroponics. It is possibly the single most important question to ask yourself before you even begin thinking about what system you want to try working with.

Hydroponics can range from extremely simple to highly complex. It all depends on your own setup, what you can afford, and how much you want to control. For example, in a more complex hydroponic garden, you would house your system indoors or in an enclosed environment, be it a specialized grow room or greenhouse, where you are able to control every aspect from temperature and humidity to light. This kind of setup is quite high-tech, where it requires gadgets and equipment such as heaters, fans, lights, and more to give you that ultimate control. It is also more advanced and best left to those who have the knowledge and experience to maintain and micromanage every aspect of their hydroponic gardens.

For the rest of us, the choice still comes down to indoors or outdoors. If you are going to grow plants indoors, it might be because we live in an apartment, or due to harsh outdoor winter weather, or just personal preference, but you probably aren't going to start out with all the gadgets of advanced indoor hydroponic gardens. There are pros and cons to having your hydroponic system indoors or outdoors. Let's take a look at the good and the bad of both options.

Sunlight: There is no better, or cheaper, source of light for your hydroponic garden than natural sunlight. Sunlight is more readily available from various angles outdoors than indoors. Some systems may even be a challenge or difficult to light properly indoors, whereas they would work well outdoors.

Space: Outdoor hydroponic gardening offers you more space to build your systems. Hydroponics is well known for allowing the growth of more plants in a smaller space than traditional gardening, which makes it ideal for small gardens or indoor gardening if you don't have a garden. However, setting up various systems indoors can be a challenge as far as space is concerned. Some systems may not be suitable for indoor gardening at all.

Affordability: Setting up outdoors means that you can spend the bare minimum on starting out. You aren't going to need extra lights or fans outdoors, whereas indoors you will need to put more thought into lighting and other aspects you may need to augment to grow plants successfully.

Pollination: Running a hydroponic garden indoors may require you to pollinate your plants manually by hand with something like a small paintbrush, whereas an outdoor system is exposed to natural pollinators like bees.

Heat: Controlling temperatures in an outdoor hydroponic system is very difficult and heat affects two aspects of your gardening: the temperature of your nutrient solution and the air temperature around your plants. Plants can take up more water in hotter conditions, which results in an excess of salts and nutrients building up in your substrate or your reservoir that affects the electroconductivity of your solution. To counter this problem, you may need to adjust your nutrient concentration in your solution. Growing plants indoors may afford you more temperature control or stability and the ability to keep temperatures from fluctuating too much.

Growing Seasons: Unlike indoor hydroponics or using a greenhouse, outdoor growing is dictated by the seasons. Therefore, you can only grow what is seasonally suitable and your growing seasons will be shorter. When growing plants indoors with appropriate temperature control, you can grow plants out of season by adding extra light and keeping your system in a warmer environment.

Pests: Pests are more abundant and have free access to your garden when you have your hydroponic system set up outdoors. While this is great for natural pollination, indoor systems have the advantage of being exposed to far fewer garden pests.

Wear and Tear: An outdoor system faces the elements outside all the time and this can lead to additional or faster wear and tear than an indoor system. UV rays from the sun are a big factor in this process.

Control: Setting up outdoors can be a great thing, but you have to relinquish a lot of control that having your hydroponic garden indoors would afford you. Lighting and temperature control aside, things like rainfall can damage your crops by flooding them or weakening your nutrient solution. You need to think carefully about the weather in your area, where you are setting up your system, and how to protect it best from adverse weather conditions when you're growing plants outdoors instead of indoors.

CHAPTER 4:

STEP BY STEP HYDROPONIC SYSTEMS

In this chapter, we're going to guide you through setting up some basic hydroponic gardening systems at home. We're going to cover four of the simpler systems, which are suitable for beginners to take on and try out.

Wick System

The wick system is possibly the easiest hydroponic system to set up and use, which makes it an ideal starting point for newcomers to hydroponic gardening.

For a very basic, single-plant wick system, refer to the passive sub-irrigation section in the previous chapter. For a slightly more complex, multiple-plant wick system, keep reading.

What You Will Need:

- Plants to grow
- Nutrient solution
- A container for your plants to grow in
- A container to act as the reservoir for your nutrient solution
- A suitable growing medium or substrate
- Suitable wick material
- Electric drill

Optional:
- Air pump, airline tube, and air stone
- Black paint

The Reservoir:

One of the simplest ways to create a reservoir is to use a rectangular tub with a lid. Using a container with a lid means that you can rest the grow tray on top of the lid. A lid will also help keep debris out of the nutrient solution and, if you're using a tub of a solid color, the light will be blocked out and prevent the growth of algae. If you are using a clear or translucent white container, you may need to paint it black to prevent light reaching the nutrient solution.

The Grow Tray:

For the grow tray, you can use another tub of the same size as the one you are using for the reservoir. However, it may be a good idea to use a shallower container if your reservoir tub is taller to let your plants see more of the world and to allow you to admire them. Ensure that your grow tray is compatible with your reservoir and that it fits comfortably and won't slide or fall off.

The Wicks:

As the wicks need to transfer water from the reservoir to the grow tray, they need to be made of a material that absorbs liquid well but won't easily rot from being wet all the time. Wicks can successfully be made from a variety of materials, including:

- Tiki torch wicks
- Strands from a mop head
- Felt strips
- Cotton rope

- Wool strips or wool rope

Air Pump:

Using an air pump in a wick system is optional. Because you are growing your plants in a growing medium, this should provide air pockets that allow your plants to take up oxygen. However, providing an oxygenated nutrient solution is always a good idea. You can purchase an aquatic air pump and air stone from a pet store.

Instructions:

1. Fill your reservoir with nutrient solution. Leave approximately a one-inch gap between the top of the solution and the lid.
2. If you are using an air pump and air stone, drill a hole in the side of your reservoir tub near the top, above the waterline, to thread the pump tube through. Once you have threaded the tube through the hole, attach your air stone and lay it at the bottom of the reservoir.
3. Drill holes into the lid of the reservoir and the bottom of the grow tray and make sure they line up. Your wicks will pass through these holes into both containers.
4. Thread your wicks through the holes in both the reservoir lid and bottom of the grow tray. Make sure that your wicks are long enough to sit comfortably in your grow medium and in the nutrient solution so that as the nutrient solution level drops the wick will be long enough to keep in contact.
5. It is a handy idea to glue your grow tray to the lid of your reservoir to create a single unit from the tray and the lid. After, seal the edges of the wick holes with silicone to prevent leaks.

6. Add your grow medium to your grow tray and plant your plants in the grow tray. Make sure to leave enough space around and between plants for them to grow to their full size.

That's it; your hydroponic wick system is done.

Deep Water Culture System

Deep Water Culture is another starter system suitable for beginners in hydroponics. These reservoirs can be made from various things, including larger containers such as buckets, tubs, or tanks, to small containers like glass jars. The type of reservoir used is dependent on the plants being grown, space available, and the preference of the gardener.

What You Will Need:

- Plants to grow
- Nutrient solution
- A container to act as the reservoir for your nutrient solution
- Net plant cups/pots
- A suitable grow medium with a decent wicking ability
- Craft knife
- Pencil
- Electric drill
- Air pump, airline tube, and air stone
- Black paint (optional)

The Reservoir:

You can use a bucket or tall tub with a lid. If you are using a clear or translucent white container for your reservoir, you may need to paint it black to prevent light from reaching the nutrient solution and thus allowing algae to grow. Using a solid-color container is helpful if you don't want to muck around with painting your reservoir.

The Grow Tray:

Unlike the wick system which has a separate grow tray, the lid of your reservoir will become your grow tray. When you are creating your deep water culture system, keep in mind the number of plants you want to grow and budget enough space around and between the plant cups for the plants to reach their full size comfortably without overcrowding.

The Air Pump:

You can purchase an air pump, air stone, and airline tube from a pet store that sells aquatic supplies. An air pump is an essential part of your deep water culture system. This is going to be a sealed system so air cannot get into your plant roots, which will make aeration of your nutrient solution important for your plants' survival.

Instructions:

1. Position the plant cups in the lid of your container according to where you are going to place them and draw a stencil around the base of the cups on the lid.
2. Using a craft knife, cut out the holes for the plant cups. You may need to adjust the size of the holes until your plant cups fit snuggly but do not fall through.
3. Fill your reservoir with nutrient solution until the solution touches the base of the plant cups. While your plants are young and in the first stages of growing, their roots will

not yet have grown down into the solution. Your wicking growing medium needs to be in contact with the solution to be able to transfer it upward to the plant until it has grown enough for the roots to hang down into the solution.

4. Drill a hole in the side of your reservoir at the top and feed your airline tube through that hole. Connect either end to the air pump and air stone and place the air stone at the bottom of the reservoir.

5. Fit the lid securely onto the reservoir, fill the plant cups with your grow medium, and plant your plants into the cups.

When using a deep water culture system with a fixed lid, it is imperative that your solution level does not drop below a level where the plant roots can reach it. To prevent this from happening when you are not around to monitor the solution level, you can either use a Mariotte's bottle or a float valve, often called a ballcock, attached to a refilling system.

When it comes time to change your nutrient solution, you can use an electrical conductivity meter to test the nutrient level. Testing the electroconductivity of the solution just means testing the strength of the solution or nutrient concentration. You use the meter to test the solution and adjust it accordingly. Alternatively, you can change it out completely on a set schedule, for instance, once a week.

Variation:

Another way of preventing the solution level from dropping too low for the plant roots to reach it is to use a floating system instead of a suspension. A floating system makes use of a raft-like way of suspending your plants on the surface of the water. You can use heavy buoyant plastic or something like Styrofoam or create a raft in whichever way that suits you. Your plants will then float on the liquid's surface and drop with the solution level, which will ensure that the roots are always in contact with the solution.

Ebb and Flow System

An ebb and flow, or flood and drain, hydroponic system is a little bit more complicated to build than a wick or deep water culture system. However, it's still suitable and achievable for those starting out.

What You Will Need:

- Plants to grow
- Nutrient solution
- A container to act as the reservoir for your nutrient solution
- A container to act as your grow tray
- A suitable grow medium
- Electric drill
- Inlet and outlet fittings or an ebb and flow fittings kit
- Submersible pump and tubing
- Analog or digital timer
- Air pump, airline tube, and air stone (optional)

- Black paint (optional)

The Reservoir:

For an ebb and flow system, a larger reservoir means that you won't have to refill it as often. Use a tall rectangular tub with a lid — a solid color works best to keep light from getting to your nutrient solution. Alternatively, you can paint a clear or translucent-white tub black.

The Grow Tray:

Use a tub with a similar base surface area as your reservoir tub, but that is shallower in height. Your grow tray doesn't need to have a lid.

Inlet and Outlet Fittings:

If you are more of a crafty, DIY person, you can go down to your local hardware store, explain your plans, and ask for advice on which fittings will best suit your needs. Alternatively, to make your life a little easier, you can purchase an ebb and flow fittings kit from a nursery or online hydroponics store.

The Submersible Pump:

You can find a submersible pump at either a nursery or some hardware stores. This is the same kind of pump used in garden water features. It doesn't need to be the biggest or best model on the market. Speak to the consultant at the store you are buying it from for advice on the correct size for your needs.

The Air Pump:

For an ebb and flow system, an air pump is optional. Your plants will be growing in a growing medium, which should provide oxygen through air pockets between the substrate particles. However, more oxygen is never a bad thing when it comes to growing big, healthy plants.

The Timer:

You can use either an analog or a digital timer, as long as it works in a 24-hour rotation. An idea is to buy a swimming pool pump timer that people use to automate their pool cleaning systems at home.

Instructions:

1. Glue the base of your grow tray to the top of the lid of your reservoir.
2. Drill holes through the lid-base combination for the inlet on one side and the outlet on the other.
3. Fit your inlet and outlet fittings to each hole and make sure they are snug and won't leak. If necessary, you can use silicone to seal them off properly.
4. Drill a hole in the side of the reservoir, near the top, above the waterline of your solution and thread the wires for the submersible pump through the hole to the outside of the reservoir. Place the pump at the bottom of the reservoir and seal the wires in place with silicone at the hole.
5. If you are using an air pump, drill another hole at the same height a couple of inches apart from the submersible pump's wire hole. Thread your airline tube through the hole and attach the air pump on the outside of the reservoir and the air stone on the inside at the bottom of the reservoir.
6. Connect the timer to the submersible pump and test it to ensure that it works correctly.
7. Fill your reservoir with nutrient solution and ensure that the level of the solution is a couple of inches below the

holes for the air pump and submersible pump.

8. Place your growing medium in your grow tray and plant your plants in the medium.
9. Place the grow tray/lid of the reservoir container on the reservoir snuggly.
10. Set your timer to activate the pump at the required regular intervals and you're done.

Nutrient Film Technique

A nutrient film technique system isn't difficult to set up. It just takes some time and planning and a little bit of space.

What You Will Need:

- Plants to grow.
- Nutrient solution.
- A container to act as the reservoir for your nutrient solution.
- Tubing or pipes to act as your grow tray
- Net plant pots/cups
- Electric drill
- Pencil
- Tubing to carry the solution from the reservoir to the grow tray channel
- Submersible pump
- Black paint (optional)
- Piping to drain the excess solution into the reservoir (optional)

The Reservoir:

The reservoir can be made from almost anything you like, from a bucket to a five-gallon drum. The choice is up to you. It is recommended to use a container of a solid color or to paint it black to prevent algae growth due to sunlight exposure of your nutrient solution.

The Grow Tray:

Unlike with other hydroponic systems, the nutrient film technique uses channels to grow the plants in. Most DIY systems make use of PVC pipes or tubes. This is so that it is more easily placed at an angle to reduce the inner surface area the nutrient solution travels along. This provides a narrow exit point for the solution so that it flows directly back into the reservoir without spilling.

The Submersible Pump:

Submersible pumps are available at hardware stores and nurseries. You are going to use the same type of pump used in water features for gardens. This does not need to be a large pump. Speak to a store consultant to help decide on the correct size pump for your needs. The rate of flow of your nutrient solution through the channel should be approximately ¼ to ½ gallon per minute. The strength of your pump needs to be able to maintain that flow rate and should be taken into consideration when you're purchasing the pump.

Instructions:

Before you start constructing your nutrient film technique system, you need to consider where you are going to set it up and what you are going to use as a frame to support the system. The grow tray channel needs to be set up at a slope of approximately 1:30 to 1:40. What this means is that for every 30 to 40 inches of the channel, the lower end needs to be dropped by one inch to create the slope. Here's an example: If you use a 40-inch long channel, the end that the solution flows out of will be one inch lower than the end the solution is pumped into. You also need to ensure that the channel stays straight all the way through. Any sagging will cause the solution to pool. Therefore, depending on the length of your channel, you may need to add additional support in sections that may sag over time.

1. Place your submersible pump into your reservoir container and measure the length of tube you will need to connect the pump to the mouth of your grow channel. When you have the right length, secure the tube to the mouth of the channel, and fill the reservoir with nutrient solution.

2. Determine the spacing of your plants and using the plant cups as stencils. Draw outlines along the top length of your grow channel. Keep in mind the space plants will need between each other to prevent overcrowding as they grow to their full size.

3. Cut or drill holes along the top of the grow channel for your plant cups and place the cups in the holes.

4. Set your channel up according to the correctly calculated slope with the lower end of the channel directly over the reservoir. It can even be touching the rim of the container. The closer the end of your channel is to the top of the reservoir, the less splashing will occur which minimizes any possible mess.

5. Place your plants in the cups and switch your pump on. You may or may not want to use a growing medium in the cups.

6. The pump should be pumping nutrient solution from the reservoir to the top end of the channel. The solution

should be flowing through the channel, making contact with the plant roots, and exiting the channel through the other end to return to the reservoir.

What you should keep in mind for this setup is that in this particular, simple design the reservoir is not covered, which allows debris and light to reach your nutrient solution. Additional steps to take to create a more enclosed system include:

- Use a reservoir container with a lid.

- Attach an elbow-shaped piece of tube or pipe to the exit end of your grow tube with a straight piece of tube that will feed directly back into your reservoir.

- Drill a hole in the reservoir lid to feed the water pump pipe through to the mouth of your grow tube and cut a hole in the lid to accommodate the downpipe from your grow tube.

CHAPTER 5:

HYDROPONIC GARDENING: NUTRIENTS

Every plant needs nutrients to survive. Traditionally, soil-based gardening plants draw their nutrients from the soil and to boost their health and growth gardeners would add manure, compost, and chemical fertilizers. However, hydroponics works differently. Without the use of soil, we need to provide the plants with all their nutrients through the solution we feed them.

Macro and Micro

There are two main categories that nutrients can be divided into. Macronutrients and micronutrients. Macronutrients are those nutrients a plant needs in large quantities. Examples of plant macronutrients include hydrogen, oxygen, potassium, and phosphorus. Micronutrients are those nutrients a plant needs only small quantities of, but they are still vital to the plant's health. Examples of plant micronutrients include copper, zinc, and iron.

If plants do not get their required amount of each nutrient, be it a macronutrient or a micronutrient, they are not able to grow and develop properly and they may not flower and bear fruit or vegetables.

PH Balance

An important factor to consider in addition to nutrients is the pH balance of your nutrient solution. This can determine the amount of nutrients your plant can absorb from the solution and thus has a big impact on its health. Your nutrient solution should be tested regularly to monitor the pH balance and adjust the solution accordingly. To adjust your pH levels, you can use a commercially bought agent that will offer a pH butter to adjust the balance for you.

Not All Plants Are Equal

Just like people, plants are different and different types of plants will require different nutrient concentrations and pH levels to support optimum health and growth. You will need to research each of the types of plants you want to grow and what their individual needs are so that you can correctly mix your nutrient solution and adjust the pH balance to suit each plant.

Temperature

When you are running an indoor hydroponic system, fluctuations in temperature, weather, and seasons aren't a big concern. When your hydroponic garden is outside, you need to consider these environmental variables.

Your nutrient solution should be kept at a consistent temperature, ideally room temperature. Room temperature is considered to be between 70 and 78 degrees Fahrenheit. If your setup is outside, you may need to consider purchasing water heaters, like the ones used in fish tanks, to keep your solution from getting too cold. During the summer months, you should be mindful to keep your reservoirs in the shade and, if necessary, use cool water when you top them up.

Buy Commercial or Make Your Own

This is a debate that can rage on for ages. Everybody has a different opinion on whether to mix your own nutrient solution at home or purchase commercially made concentration.

When buying commercial concentrations that are pre-mixed, you often buy two bottles: a bottle of macronutrients and a bottle of micronutrients. They are purchased separately because not all the ingredients, in their concentrated forms, play well with each other when thrown together in the same bottle. Some commercial nutrient packs come with several parts to offer you more control over the specific nutrient levels in your solution according to the growth phase your plants are going through.

Mixing your own nutrient solution can be tricky and requires knowledge and experience. It's not impossible, but it is very easy to get it wrong, to the detriment of your plants.

If you are new to hydroponics, you should consider starting off buying commercial nutrient concentrations. You can take your time to learn how to go about mixing your own solution at home and try your hand at it when you have more experience and knowledge.

Nutrient Ingredients

All commercially bought nutrient solutions should contain all the minerals and elements necessary for plant health.

- Potassium (K)
- Nitrogen (N)
- Calcium (Ca)
- Phosphorous (P)
- Sulphur (S)
- Magnesium (Mg)
- Iron (Fe)
- Copper (Cu)
- Manganese (Mn)

- Boron (B)
- Zinc (Zn)
- Chlorine (Cl)
- Molybdate (Mo)

Different manufacturers may vary in the exact concentration of each of these elements in their nutrient products, as there is no consensus on precise levels required. Don't worry too much about the precise concentrations but rather ensure that all of them are in the product or package you are purchasing. Some manufacturers may also include nonessential ingredients such as cobalt (Co) and silica (Si). While these additional ingredients are not life-sustaining for your plants, they can be beneficial in their growth.

Nutrient Deficiency

There are many reasons plants may become deficient in certain nutrients. These range from internal factors and climate to miscalculation of nutrients or solution strength. Let's look at what happens to your plants when they have certain deficiencies.

Nitrogen: Short plants, pale greenish-yellow leaves, and purple discoloration on the underside of tomato plant stems and leaves.

Phosphorous: Stunted growth, dark green foliage, older leaves become symptomatic first. There is a delay in plant maturation, and some plants develop a deficiency when uptake is prohibited by cold conditions as opposed to nutrient solution issues.

Potassium: Yellowed older leaves with scattered brown or black spots and the foliage tissue dies. Severely deficient plants will exhibit stunted growth and all foliage will be affected and curl.

Sulfur: While sulfur deficiency is uncommon, new foliage will become symptomatic first, displaying yellowed leaves.

Magnesium: Common in tomato plants. Leaf veins remain green with yellow areas between them.

Calcium: New foliage becomes symptomatic first with smaller, distorted leaves displaying dead spots. Root tips may die, and buds don't develop.

Iron: In contrast with magnesium deficiency, younger foliage is affected first, displaying green leaf veins with yellowing in between them.

Chlorine: Leaves wilt, are yellow, and die. These plants have stunted root growth with a thickening at the ends.

Manganese: Yellowing of the leaves between the veins, browning, and then dropping of leaves.

Boron: Smaller plant size with potential dying of growth points, ends of roots swell and discolor, eventually the plant will display brittle, thickened leaves with potential yellow spotting and curling.

Zinc: Plants are shorter, reduced length between nodes, smaller leaves that may have puckered or odd edges and potentially yellowing between the veins of the leaves.

Copper: Whilst rare, copper deficiency leads to dark green new leaves that are deformed and may have dry, brown spots.

Molybdenum: Yellowing between the veins in older foliage, which continues to newer foliage. The edges of leaves may appear scorched.

Nutrient Solution: Balance and Concentration

Nutrient solutions are about more than just getting the quantity of all the specific nutrients correct to suit a particular type of plant. It is just as important to get the concentration of the nutrients within your solution correct. You can use an electroconductivity meter to measure the concentration of your solution and match that reading to what is appropriate for your particular plants. Just as with pH and nutrient balances, you will have to research your plants and find out what each plant's ideal EC reading is.

If your EC is too high, plant growth is stunted, and your plants will lose water back into the over-concentrated nutrient solution around the roots. This usually shows itself as shorter plants with smaller leaves and a darker green color. The opposite will happen if your EC is too low; plants may take on too much water and will appear limp.

CHAPTER 6:

DISEASES, PESTS, COMMON PROBLEMS

Hydroponic gardening offers a variety of advantages over traditional soil-based gardening, but that doesn't mean it doesn't have its fair share of problems. Growing hydroponically indoors or in an enclosed environment such as a greenhouse does offer you a lot more control over setting up your hydroponic system outdoors. However, there are common issues that every hydroponic system is likely to face.

Common Problems

Water + Nutrients + Light = Algae

It's no secret that algae in your nutrient solution reservoir can be problematic. Whenever the three components that facilitate algae growth come together, namely nutrients, water, and light, it will develop. Algae is bad for your hydroponic system because with algae comes fungus gnats and when fungus gnats arrive, they will damage your plant roots.

The Fix

Prevent algae growth by making not only your reservoir but as much of your whole system as lightproof as possible. Use solid colored materials where possible. If you can't lay your hands on solid-colored materials, try painting them to block out the light. Ensure that your plant holes in your system are only big enough to fit the plant cups or pots. Any that aren't being used should be covered with a solid material that will keep light out.

Leaks

Because hydroponic systems work with a water-based nutrient solution, they can be prone to leaks developing within the system. Leaks happen for a wide range of reasons from wear and tear, to the system being clogged, and power outages that stop pumps from working.

The Fix

Check your system regularly. This will help you pick up leaks from wear and tear before they become a bigger problem. Check your drip emitters, valves, even your plant roots. You will quickly notice if a potential part of your system that has become clogged is threatening to overthrow your hydroponic garden into leakages and flooding. Make sure that your reservoir can safely hold the entire volume of the nutrient solution circulating in your system so that if a pump breaks or stops working without electricity, the reservoir won't overflow, such as with a nutrient film technique. If you are worried about the threat a power outage could pose to your plants themselves, invest in a backup power system that is battery operated and will kick in if the power goes out.

Nutrient Deficiencies, pH, EC

A nutrient imbalance can negatively affect your pH and

electroconductivity and this can occur through no fault of your own. Aside from grower error, environmental conditions can affect the uptake of nutrients and water in plants.

The Fix

Firstly, research each type of plant thoroughly and make notes of its nutrient requirements, pH preference, and ideal EC so that you can monitor the solution correctly. Temperature control and testing your nutrient solution regularly will help you monitor your solution and adjust it to keep it at the optimum level for your plants.

Hard Water

Using hard water in your hydroponic gardening system can lead to nutrient deficiencies in your plants without you realizing it. Make sure the water you are using contains no more than 200 parts per million (ppm) total dissolved solids by using a total dissolved solids (TDS) meter. The issue is that tap water has added chemicals and dissolved solids that aren't able to be absorbed by your plants and can cause your plants to be unable to take up sufficient nutrients from the solution.

The Fix

Test your water with a TDS meter to ensure it is below 200 ppm. If you are having issues with hard water, you can use an inexpensive activated coal filter to reduce the amount of dissolved solids in the water. A more expensive option is a reverse osmosis filter, which removes almost all dissolved solids.

Heat and Humidity

Heat can cause your plants to suck up more water from your solution, resulting in a nutrient concentration that is too high.

This, in turn, causes salt buildup and toxicity. Low humidity can cause plants to transpire more and lose valuable moisture from their foliage faster than they can absorb it, leading to leaf burn. High humidity can cause plants to be unable to transpire efficiently, leading to a buildup of fluids in the foliage, blossom end rot, and tip burn. High humidity also prevents the plant from moving adequate calcium up to the developing parts of the plant where it is needed, which will mimic the appearance of calcium deficiency.

The Fix

If your hydroponic system is outdoors, you can try to protect your plants from the heat by installing shade netting to provide more shade. For humidity issues, increase the ventilation and airflow both outdoors and indoors, garden fans could be an addition outdoors while regular fans and opening as many windows as possible could help indoors. If you can monitor the humidity, it should ideally be around 70–75% for most plants. If you are having low humidity problems in a grow room or greenhouse, you can try using a humidifier to increase the humidity to a more suitable level for your plants.

Plant Diseases

Just as people get sick, plants can fall ill as well. Being vigilant, checking your plant health regularly, knowing what to look for, and how to treat it can safeguard your hydroponic garden from disease.

Hydroponic gardens allow you to grow your plants closer together. They also feed off the same nutrient solution. This creates the ideal environment for disease to spread among your plants like wildfire and devastate whole gardens.

Common Diseases

Downy Mildew: Appears predominantly on the underside of leaves, does not appear powdery and is not to be confused with powdery mildew.

Powdery Mildew: Appears as a white powder sprinkled over stems and leaves.

Gray Mold: First appears as spots on leaves, progressing to fuzzy patches, which spread until the entire plant is musty and brown in color.

Root Rot: Appears as yellow, wilted plants with pulpy roots. This is caused by too many water microorganisms.

Pythium: An organism that seems like a fungus, lethal and extremely infectious.

The Solution

Clean Clothes: Diseases can hitch a lift to your indoor and outdoor hydroponic garden on your clothes. If you have been out and about, change clothes before working around your system.

Clean Up: Excess water and humidity are big culprits for the onset of mildew or mold diseases. Clean up any excess water, leaks, spills, etc. Lower the humidity by increasing airflow.

Clean Plants: Remove decaying plant matter or prune plants of any diseased foliage. Check for decay, rot in roots, and remove them immediately. Change your solution regularly to prevent the spread of disease through the recirculating solution.

These simple steps will help prevent the onset and spread of plant diseases in your hydroponic garden.

Plant Pests

Pests do not just plague traditional gardens; they also affect hydroponic plants. To ward off the enemy, you need to know what it looks like first.

Common Pests

Spider Mites: Tiny, less than 1mm in size, and may go unnoticed until the infestation is large. Check plants for webbing similar to spider webs and gently wipe the undersides of leaves with a clean tissue. Spider mite blood streaks indicate they are present.

Aphids: Green, grey, or black in appearance. They tend to congregate around stems, sucking the plant sap and weakening the plant.

Thrips: Small in size, approximately 5mm, and suck leaves dry. It can be difficult to identify, keep an eye out for little black, metallic-looking specks on the tops of leaves progressing to leaves browning and drying.

Fungus Gnats: Adult gnats are harmless, but larvae do serious damage. Larvae damage roots, stunting plant growth, and has a potential to cause bacterial infection.

Whiteflies: Tiny, approximately 1mm, moth-like appearance. Easy to see but hard to get rid of because they fly. White spots and yellowing are caused by sucking the plants dry.

Mealy Bugs: Mealy bugs are white, fluffy in appearance, and hard to get rid of because of the hard outer shell. They suck sap from plant stems.

The Solution

Beneficial Bugs: Some beneficial predatory bugs such as ladybirds and nematodes can help rid your garden of harmful pests. Ladybugs feast on aphids, for instance.

Sprays: Opt for non-harmful sprays that can be used as a deterrent or treat invasions. Avoid poisons made with harsh chemicals.

Sticky Traps: Sticky traps, similar to flypaper, will trap pests before they can get to your plants or help reduce an invasion. Yellow sticky cards draw whiteflies and fungus gnats. Blue sticky cards lure thrips.

Vigilance: Being vigilant and checking your plants regularly will help discourage an infestation from getting out of hand, especially with hard to remove pests like mealy bugs. The younger bugs can be treated with chemicals before the outer shell hardens. Adult bugs need to be removed individually using alcohol and a cotton bud.

CHAPTER 7:

TIPS AND MYTHS

Who doesn't love handy tips that make your life easier, provide you with ideas, and help you get the most out of what you're doing? In this section, we will provide you with useful tips to aid you in growing a successful hydroponic garden.

Tips for Hydroponic Gardening

Plant Selection

Not all hydroponic systems can support the same plants. It is important to select your plants according to the system you are using and how much space you have. Your choice in a hydroponic system will be determined by the space you have available to set the system up and where you are setting it up.

Start Simple

Big, beautiful hydroponic systems may look impressive and you may be aspiring to have a stunning garden. However, hydroponic gardening is all about taking it one step at a time. Start with a smaller, simpler system and grow plants that are easy to look after and grow. As you gain experience, knowledge, and confidence, you can expand and build up to bigger, better things. Hardy herbs are an excellent choice to start with. If you are unsure, ask your local nursery for their suggestions of which plants to start with in your hydroponic garden.

Growing Season Guide

As you grow your plants, observe and take note of the changes they undergo at different phases of growth and how long these phases last. This will help you compile a guide for future growing seasons.

pH and Deficiencies

When you notice a deficiency in your plants, make testing and adjusting your pH balance your first call to action to fix the problem. Many deficiency issues can easily be solved by fixing your pH because an incorrect pH can lead to plants being unable to take up the necessary nutrients effectively.

The Root of a Problem

Regularly check the roots of your plants. The roots are the most important aspect of your plant health. Without properly functioning roots, the plant cannot acquire the correct nutrients and oxygen for optimal growth. Check for damage, pests, infection, etc. to maintain a healthy root system and thus a healthy plant.

Light Up Their Life

Light is an important source of energy for plants. Without light, they cannot photosynthesize and cannot grow. If you are growing your hydroponic garden outdoors, consider the needs of the plants you are growing. Do they need full sun, partial sun, afternoon shade, or full shade? Once you know the light requirements, you can determine where best to position your system for the best light exposure. If you are growing your garden indoors, consider how much natural light the room gets. If there is not enough light to meet the plants' needs, you may consider employing additional lighting to help give them enough light.

Outdoor Elements

Outdoor hydroponic gardens that are not in a greenhouse will be subject to the elements. You may need to find ways to help shelter your plants from the heat, cold, wind, etc. such as using shade netting for shade or as a windbreak, using garden fans, and other ways to help protect them.

Temperature

When you are growing your plants indoors or in a greenhouse, try to keep the temperature as constant at the optimal temperature for your choice of plants. This will help them grow better and faster, and if you are going to grow all year round, trick your plants into thinking that all year is growing season. Keeping your nutrient solution at a constant temperature will also help convince the plants that there is no such thing as winter or being 'out of season'.

System Cleaning

You should be cleaning your hydroponic system regularly to help ward off contamination, which can lead to unhealthy plants. You should aim to clean your reservoir every two to three weeks. Clean any solid residue build-up in tubes and on the reservoir walls. Clean out the grow trays between every growing season if you are growing plants like lettuce which require new plants to grow every grow season. To clean your reservoir or system parts, use a 10% bleach solution and rinse thoroughly afterward.

Hydroponic Myths Busted!

Hydroponics is shrouded in its fair share of myths and misconceptions. Let's bust some of the most common myths about growing a hydroponic garden.

It's Unnatural

This couldn't be further from the truth. Plants grown in a hydroponic system need the same nutrients, oxygen, and environmental factors to grow and be healthy. All you are doing is removing the soil component of traditional gardening and feeding your plants the nutrients directly mixed with their water. You are not adding any harmful or artificial hormones or chemicals to your nutrient solutions.

Difficult and Complicated

As you have realized by reading this book, hydroponic gardening doesn't have to be rocket science. You can make your system as simple or as complicated as you want it to be, and that will all depend on your knowledge and experience level.

No Pesticides Necessary

As much as it would be amazing for this to be true, it's not the case. While soil-borne pests and diseases are eliminated from your worries, even indoor or greenhouse systems still fall prey to some pesky problems. Be vigilant and use as many natural or less harmful methods of prevention or cure as you can before resorting to more potent chemical warfare on bugs and illness.

It's Only Indoors

While you may have seen hydroponics being employed on a farming scale in large tunnels and greenhouses, it's available for everyone to try. Hydroponics in a controlled, enclosed environment may produce bigger, better yields, but that's not to say you can't successfully grow healthy plants for harvest outdoors.

Harmful Lighting

Stemming from the harmful lights of tanning beds, there is a misconception that grow lights used in hydroponics are harmful to you. These lights do not give off enough UV light to be harmful, just enough to grow plants when natural sunlight isn't sufficient.

CONCLUSION

As you can see from reading this book, hydroponics is easy. It's accessible to anyone, and it works. It's no more difficult than traditional soil-based gardening and anyone can do it— even kids. There are systems to cater to every growing need and different complexities to suit different experience levels from complete beginners to experienced growers. Some of the systems are more expensive to invest in, while others are much more budget-friendly. Some of these systems you can even make by upcycling old materials, recycling recyclable materials you would normally throw away, or make them from bits and pieces you may have lying around. Other basic systems need a few more resources that you will need to buy, but won't break the bank to build them.

Hydroponics is your key to soilless urban gardening in small spaces, with little or no garden, and with a small budget. You can decide how small or big you want to go, how basic or complex. The possibilities are endless. The only limit is your creativity. You can grow delicious fruits, herbs, and vegetables in your own home or garden. All you need to do is set up the most suitable hydroponics system for your space and start growing. It really is as easy as that. The best part about hydroponics is that it saves precious water and you can grow your favorites all year long in the right environment. You won't have to worry about fruits and veggies only being available in certain seasons.

So, what are you waiting for? You're armed with all the knowledge you need. Now it's time to go and build your own hydroponic system and start growing!

REFERENCES

5 Gallon Bucket DWC System. (n.d). Home Hydro System. http://www.homehydrosystems.com/system_plans/Water%20culture%20systems/5-gallon-DWC-system/5-gallon-DWC-system.html

9 Tips for Beginners Creating a Hydroponic System. (2019, May 25). Origin Hydroponics. https://originhydroponics.com/hydroponics-tips/

10 Most Common Hydroponics Pests & Diseases and How to Fight Them! (2017, May 26). Advanced Nutrients. https://www.advancednutrients.com/articles/hydroponics-plants-pests-and-diseases/

10 Myths of Hydroponics. (2011, February 11). Cocoponics. http://www.cocoponics.co/hydroponics/10-myths-of-hydroponics

15 Common Problems with Hydroponics (and How to Fix Them). (n.d.). Smart Garden Guide. https://smartgardenguide.com/problems-with-hydroponics/

20 Advantages & Disadvantages of Hydroponics That You Should Know. (2019, August 6). Green and Vibrant. https://www.greenandvibrant.com/advantages-disadvantages-of-hydroponics

Aeroponics – Benefits and Disadvantages. (n.d.). Gardening Site https://www.gardeningsite.com/aeroponics/aeroponics-benefits-and-disadvantages/

Aeroponic System. (n.d). Home Hydro Systems. http://www.homehydrosystems.com/hydroponic-systems/aeroponics_systems.html

Basic Hydroponic Systems and How They Work. (n.d.). Simply

Hydroponics. https://www.simplyhydro.com/system/

Cartwright, M. (2018, July 27). *Hanging Gardens of Babylon*. Ancient History Encyclopedia. https://www.ancient.eu/Hanging_Gardens_of_Babylon/

Commonly Found Pests and Diseases in Hydro Plants. (2017, August 1). Hydroponic Store. https://thehydroponicsstore.com/grow-blog/commonly-found-pests-and-diseases-in-hydro-plants/

Considering Common Hydroponic System Problems. (n.d.). Jason's Indoor Guide. https://www.jasons-indoor-guide-to-organic-and-hydroponics-gardening.com/hydroponic-system.html

D'Anna, C. (2019, July 22). *Ebb and Flow Systems of Hydroponic Gardens*. The Spruce. https://www.thespruce.com/hydroponic-gardens-ebb-and-flow-systems-1939219

D'Anna, C. (2019, October 14). *Hydroponic Nutrient Solution Basics*. The Spruce. https://www.thespruce.com/hydroponic-nutrient-solution-basics-1939228

Deep Water Culture (DWC) - The Definitive Guide. (n.d.). Hydro Gardeners Lab. https://hydrogardenerslab.com/deep-water-culture-guide/

Dwc Hydroponics System – The Ultimate Guide. (n.d.). Gardening Heavn. https://gardeningheavn.com/dwc-hydroponics/

Ebb & Flow (Flood and Drain) Hydroponic System. (2019, January 6). Green and Vibrant. https://www.greenandvibrant.com/ebb-and-flow-hydroponics

Espiritu, K. (2019, October 3). *History of Hydroponics: When Was Hydroponics Invented?* Epic Gardening. https://www.epicgardening.com/history-of-hydroponics/

Espiritu, K. (2019, October 3). *Hydroponics vs Soil: 7 Reasons Hydroponics Wins*. Epic Gardening. https://www.epicgardening.com/hydroponics-vs-soil/

Espiritu, K. (2019, November 30). The Nutrient Film Technique Explained. Epic Gardening. https://www.epicgardening.com/nutrient-film-technique/#Benefits_of_NFT

Fogarty, R. (2010, November 14). *Hydroponics – Static Solution Culture Technique.* https://ezinearticles.com/?Hydroponics---Static-Solution-Culture-Technique&id=5381873

Foust, Z. (2019, June 26). *Recirculating vs. Drain-to-Waste Hydroponic Systems.* Crop King. https://www.cropking.com/blog/recirculating-vs-drain-waste-hydroponic-systems

Gibs, E. (2017, August 28). *Busting Hydroponic Myths.* http://placecallhome.com/healthy-home/busting-hydroponics-myths/#Hydroponics_affect_the_environment

Grow It Best. (2019, May 23). *Hydroponic Gardening System: Tips and Tricks for Growing Plants in Hydroponic Systems.* Medium. https://medium.com/@growitbest/hydroponic-gardening-system-tips-and-tricks-for-growing-plants-in-hydroponic-systems-47c7e804a3d2

Growing Mediums and Hydroponics. (n.d). Home Hydro System. http://www.homehydrosystems.com/mediums/mediums_page.html#List_of_different_types_of_growing_media

How to Germinate Hydroponic Seedlings. (2018, December 30). PowerHouse Hydroponics. https://www.powerhousehydroponics.com/how-to-germinate-hydroponic-seedlings/

Hydroponics. (2020, April 7). In Wikipedia. https://en.wikipedia.org/wiki/Hydroponics

Hydroponics: Advantages and Disadvantages. (n.d). Dyna-Gro. https://dyna-gro.com/hydroponics-advantages-and-disadvantages/

Hydroponic Drip System Explained. (2019, January 6). Green and Vibrant. https://www.greenandvibrant.com/hydroponic-drip-system

Hydroponics Myths. (2014, March 24). Advanced Nutrients. https://www.advancednutrients.com/articles/hydroponics-myths/

Hydroponic Soda Bottle System. (n.d.). Instructables. https://www.instructables.com/id/Hydroponic-Soda-Bottle-System/

Hydroponic Wick Systems: The Training Wheels of the Hydroponic World. (2019, January 6). Green and Vibrant. https://www.greenandvibrant.com/hydroponic-wick-systems

Hydroponic Wick System – The Ultimate Guide. Gardening Heavn. https://gardeningheavn.com/hydroponic-wick-system/

Kilpinen, J. (n.d). *How to Build Your Own Flood and Drain (Ebb and Flow) System.* Just 4 Growers. http://www.just4growers.com/stream/hydroponic-growing-techniques/how-to-build-your-own-flood-and-drain-(ebb-and-flow)-system.aspx

Morgan, L. (n.d). *Nutrients – Under and Over Use.* Simply Hydroponics. https://www.simplyhydro.com/nutrients/

Morgan, L. (2020, March 6). *What's the Problem? Hydroponic Troubleshooting.* Simply Hydroponics. https://www.maximumyield.com/whats-the-problem-hydroponic-troubleshooting/2/1232

N.F.T. (Nutrient Film Technique) Systems. (n.d.). Home Hydro System. http://www.homehydrosystems.com/hydroponic-systems/nft_systems.html

Parsons W. (2020, April 20). The 15 Best Fruits, Vegetables, and Herbs for Hydroponics. https://blog.1000bulbs.com/home/15-best-hydroponics-foods

Passive Sub-Irrigation. (n.d). DIY Hydroponics Blog. https://diyhydroponicsblog.wordpress.com/hydroponic-techniques/passive-sub-irrigation/

Static Solution Culture. (n.d). Hydroponic Vegetable Garden. http://www.hydroponicvegetablegardening.com/static-solution-culture/

Stephens, O. (2019, February 14). *A Brief History of Hydroponics*. The Hydroponics Planet. https://thehydroponicsplanet.com/a-brief-history-of-hydroponics/

Stephens, O. (2019, March 15). *How to Build a Deep Water Culture System*. The Hydroponics Planet. https://thehydroponicsplanet.com/how-to-build-a-deep-water-culture-system/

Stephens, O. (2020, January 5). *Indoor or Outdoor Hydroponics? How to Decide?* The Hydroponics Planet. https://thehydroponicsplanet.com/indoor-or-outdoor-hydroponics-how-to-decide/

Sub-Irrigation System. (2019, March 30). Maximum Yield https://www.maximumyield.com/definition/3495/sub-irrigation-system

Turner, B. (n.d). *How Hydroponics Works*. How Stuff Works. https://home.howstuffworks.com/lawn-garden/professional-landscaping/hydroponics1.htm

Valdez J. (2017, March 14). The Best Crops for Raft Systems (DWC). https://university.upstartfarmers.com/blog/best-crops-for-raft-systems

What Is a Passive Sub Irrigation System? (2013, January 10). Gator Hydroponics. http://gatorhydroponics.com/what-is-passive-sub-irrigation-system/

What Is the Nutrient Film Technique - NFT? How Does It Work? (2018, December 30). Green and Vibrant. https://www.greenandvibrant.com/nutrient-film-technique

Why Coco and Run to Waste. (n.d). Glandore Hydro. https://glandorehydro.com/article/why-coco-and-run-to-waste/

Wick Systems. (n.d). Home Hydro System. http://www.homehydrosystems.com/hydroponic-systems/wick-system_systems.html

Wick Systems. (n.d). Smart Garden Guide. https://

smartgardenguide.com/what-is-wick-system-hydroponics/

BONUS!

Wouldn't it be nice to have even more motivation and inspiration on your gardening journey? As a sincere "Thank you" for reading my book, i've given you access to a FREE Indoor Gardening ebook below!

Go to This Link to Get Your Free Bonus Indoor Gardening Ebook:

bit.ly/Indoorgardeningfree

These indoor gardening tips helped me immensely with my indoor growing. I hope they help you too!

Lastly…

If you enjoy this book then I'd like to ask you for a favor. Would you be kind enough to **leave a review for this book on Amazon?**

It'd be greatly appreciated & will likely help other avid green thumbs with their projects! I read EVERY review I receive and each one helps me to serve each and every one of you better, so your feedback is highly valued!

Thank you,

Basil Green